Small Change

Small Change

by Peter Gill

MARION BOYARS
LONDON · NEW YORK

Published in Great Britain and the United States in 2008 by
MARION BOYARS PUBLISHERS LTD
24 Lacy Road London SW15 1NL
www.marionboyars.co.uk

Distributed in Australia by Tower Books Pty Ltd,
Unit 2, 17 Rodborough Road, Frenchs Forest, NSW 2086, Australia

Printed in 2008
10 9 8 7 6 5 4 3 2

A CIP catalogue record for this book is available from the British Library.
A CIP catalog record for this book is available from the Library of Congress.

ISBN 978-0-7145-2826-7

Printed in England by J. H. Haynes & Co. Ltd., Sparkford

CHARACTERS

Gerard

Mrs Harte

Vincent

Mrs Driscoll

The action takes place mainly on the East side of Cardiff.
None of the characters leaves the stage.

Small Change was first performed at the
Donmar Warehouse on April 10th 2008 with
the following cast, in order of speaking:

GERARD   Matt Ryan

MRS HARTE   Sue Johnston

VINCENT   Luke Evans

MRS DRISCOLL   Lindsey Coulson

Directed by Peter Gill
Set design by Anthony Ward
Lighting design by Hugh Vanstone

Small Change first premiered at
The Royal Court Theatre, London, in 1976.

Small Change

ONE

GERARD

It was clean. I make that up. But it was. I'll make it up. It was clean. Distempered walls with a paper border, an oval mirror, oil-cloth, a negro money-box, picture of the King... In the other house everything was worse. The smell was worse. Medals of grease on the rugs. Tea leaves and bits and leavings outside the drain, etc.... And there was a garden front and back. Two photographs show that. And I know there were roses. In one photograph, a woman standing in front of the house. In one of the photographs, a woman is standing behind an iron gate on the path in front of the house, with this bundle, this child, in this young scowling woman's arms. Thick ankles, strap shoes, a pinafore, cropped hair...

MRS HARTE

We were all young, with young families, and you could walk over the tide-field to the channel. Cut a few sandwiches for the children's tea and then when the men come home, they'd walk over and we'd all stroll back together. I don't know what we moved for – three bedrooms and a front room, and that was empty very nigh eighteen months with nothing kept in it but the bike. There was an air-strip over there during the war. I used to stand in the landing window waiting for the siren to go, and look out, nursing you old fashioned style, if I was in the house by myself. Do you remember the German plane that made a landing there? I never had such a fright in all my life. Then after that they built a big wind tunnel there. That was an awful noise too. Rover cars have got it now I'm told. Uncle picked coal over there when he was a child. You ask him. On the foreshore next to Guest Keen's. You ask him about the time he was over there with Jimmy Harrington, when my mother thought they were lost and went looking for them. And when she found them she leathered them all the way home with their wet stockings. What? Oh, he was a lovely boy, Jimmy Harrington. Oh, he really was. He was lost at sea. The war finished me off. It started everything, and it ended everything.

VINCENT

There was a wind when I turned the corner, blowing down the main road. There was no-one in front of me. It was nearly dark. Blokes from the steel works, all covered in red dust, passed me on their way home, pedalling very hard and slow against the wind. Everything went red as they tipped slag on to the foreshore. When they do that, suddenly, without a sound, the sky goes red. It was a cold night, aye, but I was soon at the corner of the street. I slung my coat over the banisters and went into the living room. Across the backs, lights through the curtains made the windows different colours. I turned on the wireless and sat down to take my boots off, putting them by the sofa. My dinner was on a saucepan being kept warm for me in the kitchen. I brought my plate in with a cloth and moved my place into the middle of the table, starting to eat before I was sat down. The potatoes were scorching. I was finished in no time. I wiped my plate clean with a bit of bread and pushed the plate away from me. Cor, the potatoes had been so hot they'd nearly burned me. Phew. I got up from the table and sat on the sofa. I didn't want to be too near the fire. I fancied a cup of tea but I felt too full from eating too quick. And too tired after work. I switched the radio over and then I switched it off. Through the wall, I could hear the wireless next door playing dance music. I went outside to the outside toilet. When I come back I could see next door's curtains weren't drawn. The music was so loud you could hear it out there. A little boy about... I don't know. Must have been about... I could see him in the room dancing to the music, all by himself, like a little girl.

	No, not like a little girl. He was just like a little boy. I watched him in the cold. It was too.
ERARD	He was sitting opposite me. He sat sprawled, legs apart, nursing a bottle of Irish whiskey inside his shirt, next to his chest. I look like my mother in every way except for her hair, he said. You've got it. He lent forward, grabbing. Where did you get it, he said. Oh Jesus... I told him.
NCENT	I eased the middle of the banked-up fire open to see its red inside and to encourage it to burn its covering of small coal. Hung over it, poker in my hand, I destroyed shapes that the burning coal was making, watched it forming a new mass, and then destroyed that. I tested my forearm, holding it before the heat. The wireless next door was still playing. I was hot. I wondered whether or not to let the fire die down. Someone had built it up to keep it in.
RS HARTE	The war finished me off. It started everything and it ended everything.
ERARD	Whose face did my grin start on? On what face will it end? I seek desperately to find resemblances – her eyes there, her manner there, her punishing, un-acknowledged, defensive aah... What is it, what is it that will, will find the moment, that will... What is it, what is it that will, will find the moment, that will... Did a woman ever live who wasn't slowly killing herself, smoothing her backside lightly as if going to sit down and saying I'm all bleeding?
RS DRISCOLL	Your legs get cold just nipping across the back like that. I'll have to go.
RS HARTE	Sit down, you've only just come in.
RS DRISCOLL	No, I can't.
RS HARTE	Come on, sit down.

MRS DRISCOLL	I mustn't be long. Oh, I don't know what to do wit myself.
MRS HARTE	Who's got the baby?
MRS DRISCOLL	I don't know what I'm going to do, I really don' *She weeps bitterly*
MRS HARTE	There we are.
MRS DRISCOLL	I kept our Eileen home. She's taken him out. Micha has gone down our Julie's.
MRS HARTE	Will you have a cup of tea?
MRS DRISCOLL	No, I can't stay.
MRS HARTE	You feel bad?
MRS DRISCOLL	I feel really bad. I'm in the middle of black-leadin the grate. I can't even work it off. He can be so ni when he wants. He was out till gone quarter to twelv last night. I don't know where he could have been that time. He was ever so abusive when I asked hin He stood in that doorway there, in that overcoa awfully unsteady. He wouldn't say. He never doe
MRS HARTE	I wouldn't give him the pleasure of asking. I shoul have been in bed if it were me. You must want yo head read, waiting up to that time.
MRS DRISCOLL	It's no good I can't go to sleep if I'm in bed on n own. And then when he's in that state I can't go sleep either.
MRS HARTE	Let mine lie by me drunk, he'd be on the oil cloth the morning.
MRS DRISCOLL	He hung his coat on a hook in the passage and near twenty pounds fell out of it.
MRS HARTE	I hope it's in yours now.
MRS DRISCOLL	Oh, I couldn't.
MRS HARTE	You should have snaffled it. How would he kno Drunken old bugger.

MRS DRISCOLL	Oh, I couldn't.
MRS HARTE	Well of all the silly, soft . . . How would he ever know? He could have lost it anywhere.
MRS DRISCOLL	I wouldn't be able to carry it off.
MRS HARTE	The two-timing, bloody, conniving old get. He wants a good kicking.
MRS DRISCOLL	I don't think you should say that kind of thing.
MRS HARTE	Well I wouldn't invite it then.
MRS DRISCOLL	I'd better be going. I'm all on edge. You won't say anything? I'm sorry. I don't know what to do. Honestly, Mrs Harte, I wish I could pack it all in.
MRS HARTE	Eh, eh, eh, eh. That's enough of that.
MRS DRISCOLL	The house is getting me down. I can't keep up with it.
MRS HARTE	Well may God forgive you.
MRS DRISCOLL	Do you know, I never used to suffer like that. Do you know, once upon a time I never knew what it was to miss a night's sleep. Now it's like hell on earth.
MRS HARTE	I know. I generally sleep all right, I must say. If I don't, it's like hell itself.
MRS DRISCOLL	I lie there. I've got this habit of clenching my hands. And sweating. I can't keep still. But you have to when he has to be up so early. It's all my fault. It's my fault. I think it's my fault, see.
MRS HARTE	What is?
MRS DRISCOLL	It *is*. Do you know . . . Well, you know, Mrs Harte, I never . . . You know . . . I never went out with anyone before I met John. Well not . . . You know.
MRS HARTE	I should hope not.
MRS DRISCOLL	The windows all need cleaning. I cleaned the mirror once today. Now there's finger marks all over it again.
MRS HARTE	Well, what does that matter?

MRS DRISCOLL	The children's shoes all need mending. *He* mend them usually. We've got a last.
MRS HARTE	Won't he do them then?
MRS DRISCOLL	Yes. Only I don't know *when* he's going to do them. just wish they was done. It's all a mess, wherever you look. You finish something. You turn around and nothing's been done. And you notice everything. get up, I think another day.
MRS HARTE	Blimey, who doesn't think that? Here goes anothe day. Let's get 'em all out of it. Let's have a sit down That's the way I think. It's wrong, I know. And the when they're gone, I get lonely. But as soon as they'r in again I think, Oh, Christ, why don't you all go ou and leave me alone.
MRS DRISCOLL	I'm all right, when I start working. If I can just ge through it, I don't know. It's wicked – to feel like this isn't it? Don't you think? It must be, I think.
MRS HARTE	What in the name of Jesus is wicked about it?
MRS DRISCOLL	Oh it is. And I used to be ever such a goo manager.
MRS HARTE	Oh don't talk so soft. Don't you think everyon feels like that, I do.
MRS DRISCOLL	And I think I'm late.
MRS HARTE	Oh now my God almighty. Are you sure?
MRS DRISCOLL	Yes. No. I don't know. I'm not certain sure.
MRS HARTE	Well then.
MRS DRISCOLL	I'm pretty sure.
MRS HARTE	Can you tell?
MRS DRISCOLL	Generally.
MRS HARTE	Well *you're* lucky. I never can. How long?
MRS DRISCOLL	I don't know.

MRS HARTE	Well, we'll hope.
MRS DRISCOLL	Yes.
MRS HARTE	Dear dear, I dunno.
MRS DRISCOLL	I'll have to go in, it's the rent man today.
MRS HARTE	I know.
MRS DRISCOLL	I owe him three weeks.
MRS HARTE	Well I don't know what I'm going to do. I think I'll be ready for the hurry-up wagon at this rate.
MRS DRISCOLL	Oh, Mrs Harte, I wish he loved me.
MRS HARTE	Don't be silly, of course he does.
MRS DRISCOLL	I think he does in his way – do you?
MRS HARTE	Don't be silly, of course he does. *As though the subject was embarrassing and out of place* Come on now, you're a young woman.
MRS DRISCOLL	If only he'd love me I'd be all right. I would. I don't care about the kids, that's the God's truth and I can't help it, I can't. I've only got any feeling for him, isn't it awful, only him. I don't want anything else in the whole world. I wish the kids were dead and me with them. It's half killing me. I followed him into town last Saturday. I left the kids with our Vincent. He's a good kid. He went right into the Park Hotel.
MRS HARTE	The mean old sod. Did you go in after him?
MRS DRISCOLL	I couldn't. I didn't have no stockings on. I only had a pair of our Eileen's school socks on. I just went out on the spur. Put my coat on over my pinafore. Who does he go to meet in a place like that?
MRS HARTE	Which bar did he go in?
MRS DRISCOLL	I don't know.

MRS HARTE   Well you were soft. I expect he just went in for a drink. You're making too much of it. You don't give yourself the chance to think about anything else. You should get out more. *Listening* There's the baby.

MRS DRISCOLL   I'll have to go in.

MRS HARTE   He'll be all right.

MRS DRISCOLL   No, I'd better go in.

MRS HARTE   Come and have a lie down in here for the afternoon.

MRS DRISCOLL   No, I'll have to get the tea on.

MRS HARTE   Oh, don't mind the tea, come in here.

MRS DRISCOLL   No, no, I'm feeling a bit better now. Thanks.

MRS HARTE   Well, bang on the wall if you want me.

VINCENT   She used to sit rubbing her ankles, pulling the curl out of her hair, and straightening it behind her ears. She used to sit as if she was warming herself. She used to sit reading her woman's paper. She used to sit, crying, bitter.

MRS DRISCOLL   I have been in worse states and I must have faith that I'll get through this one, and so on for better or worse. And that the end will be better or worse. But it will be different, being the end.

GERARD   Over the tide-field. Past dismantled allotments. Currant bushes run to seed with flowers growing in them from seed blown into them. Bits of the war. Targets. Gun posts. The sand pit. The cinder track ends in turf. Pull up a tuft of coarse grass to see if there's a curlew nest. Nothing there. That's where they lay eggs. Lie by the river. Steep, gleaming mud. Wide empty river and then in no time a full tide, swelling, catching the sun. Lie, looking up to catch a skylark. River at full flood. Slip into it. Cattle marooned on the grass island. Afraid to swim that far. Duck and float. Slide out on to the turf, and lie, hoping to catch a skylark. Then walking fast, skirting the marsh, cracking the salty reeds, walk along the trenches, cut to drain the whole field, until at last the estuary. The grasses on the bank laden with sand like snow. Watch it spread. And then the channel. The sea catching everything, swallowing everything, taking everything with it and just leaving behind a coarse rim of gritty soil. Sky goes red. When they tip slag on the foreshore, the whole place floods red. Bright weather again. Back to streets.

MRS HARTE	Where have you been?
GERARD	Over the tide.
MRS HARTE	You wanna be careful.
GERARD	Yeah.
MRS HARTE	You been swimming?
GERARD	I had a dip.
MRS HARTE	Oh don't.

VINCENT	It's all right, it's me.
MRS DRISCOLL	Is that you?
VINCENT	What?
MRS DRISCOLL	Is that you?
VINCENT	Yes. Where's the kids? Where's Eileen? What's the matter?
MRS DRISCOLL	Nothing. Where have you been?
VINCENT	There is. Mam? What's the matter? Where is everybody?

MRS DRISCOLL	Shut up. She's taken them out.
VINCENT	What's the matter then?
MRS DRISCOLL	Where have you been?
VINCENT	What is it, Mam? Come on, tell us.
MRS DRISCOLL	Where have you been?
VINCENT	I been for a swim. What's the matter?
MRS DRISCOLL	Where?
VINCENT	What is it?
MRS DRISCOLL	Where have you been?
VINCENT	Over the tide. Over the tide. All right? I been for a swim. The tide's in.

MRS HARTE	Where have you been?
GERARD	Out.
MRS HARTE	I know you been out. Where out?
GERARD	Over the East dock, for a swim.
MRS HARTE	Oh, don't. It's so dangerous.

MRS DRISCOLL	Have you been swimming?
VINCENT	Yeah.
MRS DRISCOLL	Have you been over the dock? Have you? You wait till your father comes in.

GERARD	I been over the tide.
MRS HARTE	I know, your hair's wet. Was the tide up? Was it? Eh?
GERARD	Of course it was.
MRS HARTE	I wish I had a paper, I'd look. Was it?

GERARD	Yes, I said.
MRS HARTE	It better have been.

GERARD	Where you going?
VINCENT	I got to go in.
GERARD	Oh.
VINCENT	Where YOU going?
GERARD	I got to go in.
VINCENT	Well, what's the matter with you then? Eh? Mmmm?
GERARD	I'm going in then. O.K. O.K.?
VINCENT	All right then, go in.
GERARD	You going in?
VINCENT	Yeah.
GERARD	I got to have my tea.
VINCENT	All right then.
GERARD	Call for us later then.
VINCENT	O.K.
GERARD	Don't forget. Vincent. Vincent!
VINCENT	I won't forget. Go on. I'll see you later.
GERARD	Where you going? I thought you was going in?
VINCENT	I got to do my paper round first.
GERARD	You've done your paper round.
VINCENT	I haven't. I didn't do it.
GERARD	Do you want me to come with you then?
VINCENT	No, I'm not doing it.
GERARD	Why not?

VINCENT	I don't feel like it. All right? Anyway I'm packing it in.
GERARD	Where you going then?
VINCENT	I don't know. I thought you had to go in. Go on. I'll see you later.
GERARD	No you won't
VINCENT	All right then. What's the matter with you? Eh? Mmmm? All right then.
GERARD	Nothing's the matter with me.
VINCENT	Well then, go in then.
GERARD	I am going in.
VINCENT	I'm going in an all.
GERARD	Don't go in.
VINCENT	I got to.
GERARD	And me.
VINCENT	I'll see you later.
GERARD	Aye. Don't forget.
MRS DRISCOLL	Vincent!
MRS HARTE	Come here let me look at you. Come here. Why are your shorts buttoned like that? Where have you been?
GERARD	Out playing.
MRS HARTE	I know. Where have you been?
GERARD	Out the back. Down the shelter.
MRS HARTE	Who with?
GERARD	With Vincent.

MRS HARTE	Come here.
GERARD	No.
MRS HARTE	Come here.
GERARD	*Giggling* No.
MRS HARTE	Come here, till I split you. What were you doing? Come here.
GERARD	Playing.
MRS HARTE	Come here.
GERARD	*Giggling* No.
MRS HARTE	Wait till I catch hold of you.
GERARD	With Vincent.
MRS HARTE	Come here. Gerard.
GERARD	I'm going out. Tara.
MRS HARTE	Gerard.
VINCENT	Gerard.
GERARD	What?
VINCENT	Got any?
GERARD	What?
VINCENT	Seen any nests?
GERARD	I'm stuck.
VINCENT	What d'you mean?
GERARD	Are you stuck?
VINCENT	Of course I'm not stuck. What do you mean stuck? How can you be stuck? I've just stopped that's all.
GERARD	Don't look down. I'm stuck.
VINCENT	What? Blimey. Come down, come down.

GERARD	I can't.
VINCENT	Oh, blimey.
GERARD	Don't come up.
VINCENT	Blimey. Well climb on up. Go on.
GERARD.	I can't.
VINCENT	Well, come on down.
GERARD	I can't.
VINCENT	Blimey. It was you went up there. You went up there. What do you want to go up there for?
GERARD	Don't look down.
VINCENT	Why not? *He looks down* Blimey!
GERARD	Here's the dock coppers.
VINCENT	Oh Christ. Come on. Come down.
GERARD	I can't.
GERARD	Or earlier. Lost, crawling up the beach, under the legs of tethered beach ponies. Short beaten horses. Shore, ribbed like the roof of a huge mouth. The grey sea filling abandoned holes. Ma ma ma Mam...
MRS HARTE	What have you got there? What have you got in your hand? Come on – give it to me. Sweet paper. Throw it down. I'll slap you hard. Here hold my bag.
VINCENT	You coming over the field, Ger?
GERARD	No, I can't.
VINCENT	Why not?
GERARD	I can't get through the barbed wire.
VINCENT	Yes, you can. Come on.

MRS DRISCOLL   Where have you been?

GERARD   Perhaps I'd been over the park, or into town, or with Vincent, or out, or lying under the tree. Or down the field, lying under the tree, eating banana sandwiches or hanging about or deliberately wasting time, deliberately creating tedium. Or over the park, having squeezed through the railings rather than go through the gate, and having squeezed through the railings, climbed up and sat on the railway embankment, above the bushes and birch trees, and looked down on to the soccer pitches and having walked along the line above the playground, sat above the other pitches and seen the whole plan of the park. Or gone for a swim in the park baths. Through the green turnstile, hoping for a single cubicle, to avoid other boys. Boys changing in cubicles without doors. Boys with lamed legs. Boys flicking towels. Afraid to stand near the deep end, for fear of being pushed in. Grazed knee on the concrete of the pool. Was the sting from the chlorine or the concrete grazing the skin off? Polio scares. Or over the playground. Sometimes the swings are wrapped round the top of the supports by the big boys, youths, thugs, Teds, youths, roughs, vandals now. Swinging, frightened someone will push you so high that you have to jump off or it's too late and you are afraid to jump off. There's a moment when the swing stops, with a curious kind of gulp in the chain. You could go so high you could swing right over and crash down. The older boys are standing on the seats, girls sitting between them, between their legs and feet, bending at the knees to get an impetus to swing higher. The Parkie driving them away. Cheeking him. Hooligans. I forgot.

VINCENT   Do you want a lift, Gerard?

MRS HARTE   You're not giving him a lift. I've told you two before. About that. On the handle bars. I saw you.

VINCENT	Only on the bar, Mrs Harte.
MRS HARTE	No.
GERARD	No, you go on. I'm not going this afternoon.
MRS HARTE	What did you say?
GERARD	You heard.
MRS HARTE	What did you say?
GERARD	You heard that, too.
MRS HARTE	Come here, I'll cleave you, you little get.
GERARD	I'm not feeling well. I can't go back.
MRS HARTE	On your way. And you too, Vincent. Off you go.
GERARD	I'm not going.
MRS HARTE	You are.
GERARD	I'm not.
MRS HARTE	Oh oh, but you are.
GERARD	Oh, but I'm not.
MRS HARTE	Now, get your blazer.
GERARD	I feel sick.
MRS HARTE	So do I. Where is it?
GERARD	Blazer!
MRS HARTE	That's a nice blazer.
GERARD	You wear it, then.
MRS HARTE	Come here.
VINCENT	I'm going, then.
GERARD	Yeah. You go on.
MRS HARTE	He's coming now, Vincent. Get your blazer. Now get it.
GERARD	I don't know where it is.

MRS HARTE	Find it. Upstairs.
GERARD	It isn't upstairs.
VINCENT	I'm going then.
MRS HARTE	I'm not writing you a note, so don't think I am.
GERARD	That's O.K. by me.
MRS HARTE	You're a hateful kid.
VINCENT	Tara.
GERARD	Anyway I'm leaving.
MRS HARTE	I wish you could bloody leave. The sooner the better. But you're not leaving. Right. Dear dear. You'd better go, Vincent.
VINCENT	Tara then.
GERARD	What's the matter?
VINCENT	I'm going then.
GERARD	What's the matter?
MRS HARTE	Nothing's the matter. I'm sick of you, that's all, you little swine. I am. Honest to God, I am. You're tiring me out.
GERARD	All right, I'll go.
MRS HARTE	I don't care if you do go.
GERARD	All right, I'm not going.
MRS HARTE	And I'm not writing you a note.
GERARD	Don't worry I'll write one myself.
MRS HARTE	Oh, Jesus, help me with this swine of a kid.
VINCENT	I'm going then.
GERARD	Look at it.
MRS HARTE	What?
GERARD	All of it. In here. Out there. The street. I'm fed up.

I'm fed up.

MRS HARTE   You're fed up. That's a laugh. You're bloody fed up. A kid of your age. I'm fed up to the back teeth, I am.

GERARD   *And* I'm bored.

MRS HARTE   Bored. What you bored with then? Eh? Eh?

GERARD   Oh, nothing, nothing. I'm going.

MRS HARTE   Where?

GERARD   Oh, I don't know. School.

MRS HARTE   You'd better run for it then.

GERARD   Or perhaps I'd been over the park. Seen the old man with his plastic shopping-bag and sandwiches for his favourite children. Or gone down the other end, the nice end, with the dilapidated tennis courts and garden and bowling-green fielding old men with flannels and cream jackets and rubber over-shoes, with their rubber mats. Boring, unavoidable, glimpses of peace, with their gardens, and allotments, pipes. Unendurable visions of their perfect lives. Gardens, cars, good sense, polished furniture, kindliness. Their dullness and their humour killing me. Clerks in the Inland Revenue, with established posts or perhaps retired, with daughters and a son with a car. Holidays. Two weeks. Rockeries. Kindly good sense. Delivered papers. *Everybodies, News Chronicle, Herald. Reynolds News*? Hardly. Perhaps. Radio with pleated silk, backing the fretwork. Anonymous, once pretty wives. With their prudence and irritating passions and have been in the war.

MRS DRISCOLL Aren't you going out, Vincent? Vincent?

VINCENT   No.

MRS DRISCOLL Don't you have to go to church tonight?

GERARD	Don't forget I'm on the altar tonight, Mam. Mam.
VINCENT	No.
MRS HARTE	What?
GERARD	Don't forget will you?
MRS HARTE	*Imitating his whine* Don't forget.
MRS DRISCOLL	Well don't sulk in here, Vincent.
GERARD	I wants a clean cotta mind.
MRS HARTE	Do you? Well you can want on.
GERARD	Or, Mam.
MRS DRISCOLL	Stop spitting, Vincent. There's a good boy. It's a terrible habit you've got. Are you sure you're not meant to be going to church?
GERARD	Mam.
MRS HARTE	You had it clean on on Sunday. Anyway you didn't bring it home in time.
GERARD	I did. I brought it home yesterday.
MRS HARTE	Yesterday.
GERARD	Well, will you iron it then?
MRS HARTE	No I won't bloody iron it. On your way.
MRS DRISCOLL	It's Wednesday night, Vincent. I'm sure you're supposed to be in church.
MRS HARTE	And I'm not washing any more football gear either. Right?
GERARD	Right.
MRS HARTE	You cheeky ... Come here. Come here, till I kill you.
MRS DRISCOLL	Vincent.
VINCENT	Oh Christ. I'm going out.
MRS DRISCOLL	What did you say? Vincent.

VINCENT	Tara.
MRS DRISCOLL	Vincent. What did you say, Vincent!
MRS HARTE	Come here.
MRS DRISCOLL	Vincent!
MRS HARTE	There's Vincent. Come in, Vincent. You going to benediction? If you are I hope you're in a better frame of mind than him.
VINCENT	No.
MRS HARTE	I bet he doesn't keep on about clean cottas.
GERARD	Why don't you do a swop?
MRS HARTE	I wish to Christ I could.
GERARD	Anyway, he doesn't need a clean cotta, that's why.
MRS HARTE	Because he keeps his clean, I should think.
GERARD	No, clever, he got chucked off.
MRS HARTE	Get out he never did, did you, Vincent? What for?
GERARD	His face don't fit.
MRS HARTE	Now, shut it you. There's favouritism down there. Right through the bloody parish. Nice Catholics some of them are.
GERARD	That's what I said.
MRS HARTE	I'll do for you in a minute.
GERARD	Come on. Come on.
MRS HARTE	Now stop it.
GERARD	Come on.
MRS HARTE	Go on, go on. Get out, get out. Ooh, I've hurt my arm now.
GERARD	Have you? Come on. What's the matter.
MRS HARTE	I'm not talking to you.

GERARD   Why not?

MRS HARTE   You've got no respect. Go on the pair of you.

GERARD   Where you going?

VINCENT   I'll walk down with you.

MRS HARTE   And don't you be late. Do you hear?

GERARD   We're going for chips.

MRS HARTE   You are not.

GERARD   Tara.

MRS HARTE   Do you hear me?

VINCENT   Let's go down the park.

GERARD   The gate'll be shut.

VINCENT   Let's go over the warmies.

GERARD   Or. No.

VINCENT   Let's go over the white-washed wall.

GERARD   What for?

VINCENT   I don't know.

GERARD   Let's go over the park.

VINCENT   Come on then. We'll climb over. Come on.

GERARD   No. The Parkie'll see us.

VINCENT   No he won't. We'll climb over.

GERARD   I can't.

VINCENT   We'll squeeze through. You're skinny enough.

GERARD   The afternoon was... It's evening anyway, almost
            very near. The afternoon... It was evening, it was
            evening. Late afternoon. Got out of bed. This is
            intolerable. And picked up a milk bottle. Stop. Went
            round the room collecting up milk bottles, pouring all

the milk I found, into one. 'Ere that's gone off. Phew, I'm not surprised. There. Took a bottle of white medicine off the mantlepiece, uncorked it and took a swig. No. I put it back. There was nothing outside the window and nothing when I opened the door. If I smoked I could be lighting another cigarette, finger shaking, holding the cigarette and a cup of coffee in the one hand. Laid my head on the table. Don't go to sleep. Picked up my trousers off the floor and put them on. There we are. I wish I hadn't done that. I sat down and put my head on the table again. Where was I? You're dying, talking, experience hoarded is death. Thou shalt not take to thyself any graven thing nor the Likeness of anything which is in the Heavens above or in the earth beneath. Thou shalt not adore them nor serve them.

MRS HARTE   I could lend you ten bob.

GERARD   Thanks, that'll be fine.

MRS HARTE   Now I want that back remember?

GERARD   Don't you always?

MRS HARTE   You got me heart scalded. Why don't you settle down? Job to job. What do you do up there anyway?

GERARD   What I do up there is I walk the streets.

MRS HARTE   You'll come to grief.

GERARD   I have quite literally.

MRS HARTE   What have you got to be sorry for?

GERARD   That's it.

MRS HARTE   You ought to have my worries.

GERARD   I do.

MRS HARTE   I wish I could afford...

GERARD   Money money money.

MRS HARTE	You'll be the finish of me. You will.
GERARD	You'll see to that, won't you?
MRS HARTE	Honest to my God, isn't it terrible?
GERARD	Sorry. Sorry. Sorry.
MRS HARTE	If anyone's heart is broke it's mine.
GERARD	Don't start.
MRS HARTE	He was ill and I couldn't go up to him. Others went. I couldn't. I knew he wouldn't mind. No-one expected me to by then, anyway. Then he died. Oh well.
VINCENT	Where is he?
MRS DRISCOLL	Who?
VINCENT	Him.
MRS DRISCOLL	I don't know.
VINCENT	Mmmn.
MRS DRISCOLL	Gone for a drink – don't ask me.
VINCENT	Where's my dinner?
MRS DRISCOLL	Sit down, don't panic, it'll be here.
VINCENT	I haven't got long.
MRS DRISCOLL	I know. I bet it's cold on the dock today.
VINCENT	It is.
MRS DRISCOLL	Did you see your father down there this morning?
VINCENT	Aye. Only for a second.
MRS DRISCOLL	I wonder when he'll be in.
VINCENT	*Yawning* I don't know. That's what I said.
MRS DRISCOLL	What's the matter with you?
VINCENT	What do you mean?

MRS DRISCOLL	You've got 'em on you all of a sudden haven't you? Come on sit to the table. Haven't you got a fag?
VINCENT	No.
MRS DRISCOLL	What did you do with the five I bought you yesterday?
VINCENT	Smoked 'em haven't I.
MRS DRISCOLL	Well I don't know what a boy of your age wants smoking for any road.
VINCENT	No?
MRS DRISCOLL	What's up?
VINCENT	I don't know.
MRS DRISCOLL	There's something up.
VINCENT	No there isn't.
MRS DRISCOLL	If it's about finishing your time. You're finishing it, your time.
VINCENT	Well, I'm not finishing my time.
MRS DRISCOLL	You are finishing your time.
VINCENT	I'm not finishing my time.
MRS DRISCOLL	Vincent, don't, my nerves are bad this morning. You'll have to work your time. Don't be silly, Vincent.
VINCENT	Well I'm not. I'm sick of not having any money. Aren't you? Don't you want any more money?
MRS DRISCOLL	Yes.
VINCENT	And I'm sick of having it thrown in my face.
MRS DRISCOLL	What?
VINCENT	Not bringing much money in. It's not my fault.
MRS DRISCOLL	Who said it was? What a thing to say. When did I

throw it up at you, Vincent? What an awful thing to say.

VINCENT   Well?

MRS DRISCOLL   When?

VINCENT   Friday. Last Friday you did. Practically every Friday. Well I'm packing it in. It's a big fiddle anyway.

MRS DRISCOLL   What is?

VINCENT   Down there. I know the trade. Well I practically do. I can do as good a job as most fellas any road. Except for one or two of them.

MRS DRISCOLL   You don't know how lucky you are, that's your trouble. How many boys have got a trade? Tell me that.

VINCENT   How many wants one?

MRS DRISCOLL   Don't be silly.

VINCENT   It's bloody antique.

MRS DRISCOLL   What did you say?

VINCENT   It's antique. The yard is practically at a standstill. It's an antique system anyway, having to be put in for a trade. It's all a fiddle.

MRS DRISCOLL   How's it a fiddle?

VINCENT   What? It's not a fiddle you keeping me on practically nothing for seven years, while they get free labour and skilled work, and then a skilled man at the end of it?

MRS DRISCOLL   Don't talk so stupid.

VINCENT   It's true.

MRS DRISCOLL   Well, if you want to look at it that way.

VINCENT   That's the only way to look at it.

MRS DRISCOLL	It's not the only way to look at it. I don't know. I don't see how it's a fiddle. It's a fair exchange to me. Look what your father would have done for a trade, but they were too poor and he had to bring in what he could.
VINCENT	I can get a job doing what I'm doing now.
MRS DRISCOLL	Don't be silly. They want skilled men.
VINCENT	I am a skilled man. I know the trade near as makes no difference.
MRS DRISCOLL	Don't be so big headed, Vincent. It doesn't become you. You'll have to serve your time. You'll have to have signed indentures. I read it every night in the *Echo*. Only time served men need apply.
VINCENT	Not for everything.
MRS DRISCOLL	*You* count yourself lucky.
VINCENT	Why should I?
MRS DRISCOLL	Why should you? Because you are. How many apprentices are there down the Mount Stuart? Go on tell me. And how do you think you're one of them?
VINCENT	Oh go on. That's right. Throw it up.
MRS DRISCOLL	Not through your father, that's for sure.
VINCENT	No, through yours. Go on.
MRS DRISCOLL	My father was a really skilled man and don't you forget it. Bloody Catholics.
VINCENT	What?
MRS DRISCOLL	Bloody Catholics with your religion and your Labour Party. You're all voice.
VINCENT	Better than no voice at all. It's a wonder you don't vote like him an' all. I don't think you think you should vote. You don't vote do you?
MRS DRISCOLL	No. I don't see the point in women voting.

VINCENT	Nor me.
MRS DRISCOLL	I can't bear all this talk. I don't know anything and all I hear is talk. It wears me out.
VINCENT	I'm not just talking. I'm packing it in.
MRS DRISCOLL	Vincent, that's not doing anything.
VINCENT	Well, why don't you do something? Why don't you stand up to him? Why do you pick on me? You just want to be a slave, you do.
MRS DRISCOLL	I never wanted all this. I never came from all this.
VINCENT	What's wrong with it? This is nice. You keep it smashing, Mam.
MRS DRISCOLL	I don't want you down them yards. But what say do I have?
VINCENT	Why not? It's great down there. It is.
MRS DRISCOLL	Is it? I don't know. I don't know anything. Except I've heard of boys of fourteen running home because of the awful noise. But it's not for me to know. But I do know it's good to have a trade. You wanted to leave school.
VINCENT	I never did. You made me.
MRS DRISCOLL	We didn't. What good was another year's schooling going to do you, eh? You wanted to leave.
VINCENT	Well, I'm packing it in all right?
MRS DRISCOLL	Stop it, Vincent, my nerves are awful bad.
VINCENT	You see you always do that. Why can't you be on my side, Mam. You see. Aah. It's all right. Don't bother.
MRS DRISCOLL	He's grieving. I'd come if I could. He's grieving. He's never been a scrap of trouble to me, and I'd love to help him. I'd get out of this if I could. It's my fault I know. I'd come if I could.

GERARD	The sun's blinding me.
VINCENT	Well close your eyes then.
GERARD	I'm testing them.
VINCENT	We ought to go in while the tide's up.
GERARD	I'm too hot. Hey is that a skylark?
VINCENT	Don't be soft, of course it isn't.
GERARD	Well, what is it then? It's high enough up.
VINCENT	I don't know what it is. It's not a lark, that I do know.
GERARD	How do you know?
VINCENT	Look, it's not a skylark.
GERARD	Look, the moon's gone in .
VINCENT	Well?
GERARD	I don't know what time it is. I'll get murdered.
VINCENT	Nor me. The pubs are out . . . listen . . . I'll get done.
GERARD	And me. Look.
VINCENT	What?
GERARD	Look up there.
VINCENT	What? What at?
GERARD	Light has the fastest speed right. Faster than sound.
VINCENT	Of course, it's faster than sound.
GERARD	That's what I said. Look up there then. You looking?
VINCENT	Yeah.
GERARD	I can't see you.
VINCENT	I'm looking.
GERARD	I wish the moon would come out.
VINCENT	Why?

GERARD	Now, take any star.
VINCENT	Is this a card trick?
GERARD	No listen. Now a star, X distance from the earth is, when seen by us, Y times in its past. Right?
VINCENT	So what?
GERARD	Do you agree?
VINCENT	Aye.
GERARD	So that the world being X distance from the star would therefore from the star's point of view be Y times in its past. Do you agree?
VINCENT	Nah. Well, in the idea.
GERARD	So if we were up there, we could be seeing, well, we, we'd be seeing anything. Something in the past, any road.
VINCENT	What?
GERARD	Something. Depends. Something. Pyramids. Anything. Something. A man's life must be in existence for all time, this must be.
VINCENT	What for? What about time though?
GERARD	What?
VINCENT	Doesn't it have an end?
GERARD	Dunno. I reckon not.
VINCENT	Anyway, that's all just an idea.
GERARD	What do you mean just an idea?
VINCENT	Well, I can't take it seriously.
GERARD	Why not?
VINCENT	You can't prove it.
GERARD	Of course you can prove it. I just have.

VINCENT	That's you, see. You want an easy solution, so it's all fixed. You can't prove an idea.
GERARD	Of course you can. Of course you can prove an idea. What do you mean you can't prove it?
VINCENT	Prove it then. I'd need evidence.
GERARD	They could prove it.
VINCENT	How?
GERARD	With a machine.
VINCENT	What machine?
GERARD	I don't know. You're supposed to be good with your hands, you ought to be able to think of something.
VINCENT	Well I can get the chain back on my bike without having a breakdown.
GERARD	So can I get the chain back on my bike. I just can't mend a puncture. But I can get the chain back on my bike.
VINCENT	Not without having a nervous breakdown, you can't
GERARD	It's true enough, I bet, what I said.
VINCENT	It's just an idea. They'd need a machine. And if they did make a machine, you couldn't prove it.
GERARD	Why not?
VINCENT	Because human life isn't long enough. You'd be dead before you got there.
GERARD	Not if they got one to go fast enough. Got you.
VINCENT	Nah. They'll get to the moon though. You watch it. Journey into space.
GERARD	They won't will they?
VINCENT	You don't like that do you. What's the time then?
GERARD	I don't know.

VINCENT	We'll get done. The moon's out again.
GERARD	Look at it.
VINCENT	What?
GERARD	The sun.
VINCENT	Why?
GERARD	To test your eyes.
VINCENT	What do you want me to go blind? You're up the wall, you are.
GERARD	Isn't it hot? Coming in?
VINCENT	Nah. Don't you go in either.
GERARD	Why not?
VINCENT	It is a lark and all. Two of them.
GERARD	I'm going in.
VINCENT	The tide's on the turn. Look at it. You can't go in now.
GERARD	I don't care.
VINCENT	Don't be daft, you know how fast it goes out.
GERARD	I'm only going for a dip.
VINCENT	Don't be so bloody daft, Gerard.
GERARD	I'm only going in for a dip.
VINCENT	No. Don't be so bloody daft, Gerard.
MRS DRISCOLL	Oh, Mrs Harte, I felt as if I didn't exist. I kept looking out of the window and I couldn't work out how it could be possible. It's easy to say so now, because although I think it, I don't know it, if you can take my meaning. And the line and the line post and everything. Well the truth to tell I got very frightened, so I locked the bedroom door and I lay on

the bed. But I couldn't stop my heart thumping. I was really frightened, and I got so far down into myself I felt I should never come back and I got into a real fright and I thought I must work this off but I couldn't bear to have the baby near me or to have to talk to our Colin so I slipped right out of the back door. I got down the gully all right, but when I came out on the main road I didn't know where I was and this feeling. Oh my God you wouldn't credit it. I felt as if I was... Even now you're here and you're not here. Isn't it dreadful? Oh what ever am I going to do?

MRS HARTE   It's not as if we've got a bit of brandy. It's terrible to be poor.

MRS DRISCOLL   Oh Jesus ... Oh dear. *She laughs* In the street Mr Riley took my arm and I felt a bit better. He's such a gentleman. Do you ever get this feeling? It's awful. It's happening, but how can it be happening? Like I feel as if I'm not here. I feel as if I don't exist at all. How can I exist? Now I'm just saying that. That's what I felt like. I can't go on like this. I'm not going to shout, but it won't go away.

MRS HARTE   Come on, love.

MRS DRISCOLL   Go away.

MRS HARTE   Come on.

MRS DRISCOLL   No.

MRS HARTE   Yes, come on, come on, come on, my love.

MRS DRISCOLL   Don't make it worse. I'll settle down. Don't worry about me. Oh Oh. I'll have to go back. I can't stand still.

MRS HARTE   You just try.

MRS DRISCOLL   Thank you.

MRS HARTE   Dear, dear, dear. You stay in here. Gerard'll pop in next door and see everything is all right. You come and lie in here, my love.

MRS DRISCOLL   I'm awfully sorry.

VINCENT   Is my mother in here?

MRS DRISCOLL   Yes. I won't be long. Go on. Isn't it terrible. Vincent!

MRS HARTE   Hello, Vincent.

MRS DRISCOLL   Go on. I'll be in in a minute.

VINCENT   They want their tea.

MRS DRISCOLL   It's all ready. I'll be in in a minute.

MRS HARTE   Go on, son. She'll be in.

VINCENT   Michael's crying.

MRS DRISCOLL   I know, I can hear him can't I?

VINCENT   Look Eileen's got to go out.

MRS DRISCOLL   Go in, go in, will you?

MRS HARTE   Go on, son.

VINCENT   Why doesn't she come in?

MRS HARTE   She'll be in.

VINCENT   Our Dad's in.

MRS DRISCOLL   He's not is he?

VINCENT   No, he isn't.

MRS DRISCOLL   What did you say that for?

VINCENT   Because he will be in. He should be in.

MRS DRISCOLL   Vincent. Vincent! Vincent! *Screaming* Come here! Oh dear, oh dear, oh dear.

MRS HARTE   She was a strange girl. Poor girl. And him, he's as ignorant as they come. Like your grandfather Harte. Bloody Bible punching old get. Your grandmother wanted her hair cut when we all did because she used to get so hot in that kitchen with that big range. He wouldn't allow it. He said a woman's hair is her crowning glory, as if the bloody Bible said what length. Ignorant old bigot. I'd have cleaved him open. Bloody Bible punching old get. Like him next door, and he's nothing to write home about. She says she can't find no love in her for her kids and yet look how she keeps them. I wish I had a quarter of her energy. And she sends him to church and to a Catholic school. She's a damn sight better than half of them that go. She's a strange girl. She comes from a lovely family. You should see her sister's home. *She*'s a smart woman. And he's years older than her. I don't know whatever she saw in him. I can't bear him. Heavy, big, dark thing he is.

GERARD

Rattling through my dry mind like peas or lentils or rice blown through my fingers, across the pane and across my eyes the grasses' tops are thrown. The fields are nervous, their contents quivering. Field after field after field, all shaking with nerves. I'm exhausted looking out of train windows. I'd like to jump out of here at this speed, and retain this speed's magic freedom, unhampered by the moquette seating and that cream and green ceiling and grubby walls and those pictures of the pump room Llandrindod Wells and pictures of Burnham-on-Sea, and fly out on a kite string, and describe in the air currents and shapes, determined by the train's speed, going and never arriving and feel the occasional tough jerk at the end of my tether, reminding me of restrictions, but feeling its immediate release, billowing me out to freedom and safety and purpose.

MRS HARTE

I wish I could come up when you're ill like that. What did you get ill like that for? I nearly died with worry – you up there and I can't get up to you. How are you?

GERARD	Oh much better.
MRS HARTE	Are you feeling any better?
GERARD	Oh much.
MRS HARTE	You had me worried to death. How did you get ill like that? What were you doing?
GERARD	Nothing.
MRS HARTE	You must have done something to get ill like that.
GERARD	Nothing.
MRS HARTE	You ought to have stopped in the army that time. That's what you ought to have done. You had a good career ahead of you there. You gave up an easy billet there.
GERARD	Literally.
MRS HARTE	In the Far East. It would have killed me. You're drifting away from me. I feel a dead failure . . . I wish I could come up when you're ill like that. Are you feeling better?
GERARD	Much.
MRS HARTE	If anything happened to you, I'd lose my mind. When you ran away I was so frightened.
GERARD	What do you mean, ran away? I never ran away.
MRS HARTE	You just slammed out of the house. Now I think you've run away for good haven't you?
GERARD	I'm here aren't I?
MRS HARTE	But you're drifting away from me.
GERARD	I can't stay here. I hate it.
MRS HARTE	Not as much as me. I can tell you.
GERARD	Come back with me.
MRS HARTE	I wouldn't fit in up there.

GERARD	Come back with me. I'll find a place.
MRS HARTE	I'd love it, but it's not to be.
GERARD	Why?
MRS HARTE	Don't ask me, son. That's how it is. I wish I could cry like that.
GERARD	Silly isn't it.
MRS HARTE	Yes.
GERARD	Come with me please. Oh please. Let's run away together. You and me. For Christ's sake don't cry, Mam, it will kill me.
MRS HARTE	I don't cry.
GERARD	Oh Jesus, you're crying.
MRS HARTE	I'm not crying.
GERARD	I am.
MRS HARTE	I'm not.
GERARD	Nor am I, now.
MRS HARTE	I never cry.
GERARD	I don't much. Never.
MRS HARTE	You always used to cry.
GERARD	You don't cry.
MRS HARTE	No. Leave that to everyone else, I'm sorry I couldn't come up to see you. But you must know me by now. Too much of a coward.
GERARD	I didn't expect it.
MRS HARTE	What do you mean?
GERARD	That I didn't expect you to come up.
MRS HARTE	What's that supposed to mean?
GERARD	What I said.

MRS HARTE You can be cruel sometimes.

GERARD Can I?

MRS HARTE When you going back?

GERARD I don't know.

MRS HARTE I expect I'll see you sooner than I think I will.

GERARD The trees closed like fir cones as the train sped under them and they receded. The sun made a hot ring in the clouds, like its reflection through a magnifying-glass on the back of your hand or on paper you want to burn. The train went through the countryside as if it would break the weather. Smoke from a fire stained the air above a whole field. It began to get cooler and look greener. There were dark patches in the fields. It was as if huge animals had been sleeping in them.

MRS HARTE I couldn't get you out of my sight at one time, now I think you've run away for good.

GERARD What say?

MRS HARTE You're drifting away from me.

GERARD I'm here aren't I?

MRS HARTE But you're drifting away from me.

GERARD I can't stop here, I hate it.

MRS HARTE Not as much as me, I can tell you.

GERARD Let's blow it up.

MRS HARTE Come here. Keep still. You're going grey.

GERARD What you... Don't!

MRS HARTE How old are you. Keep still. When I was your age I had three or four kids.

GERARD Come back with me.

MRS HARTE   I wouldn't fit in up there.

GERARD   Come back with me. I'll find a place.

MRS HARTE   I'd love it but it's not to be.

GERARD   Why not, why not?

MRS HARTE   Why? Don't ask me, son. That's how it is. I wish I could cry like that.

GERARD   I'm all right, I'm tired of the train. Silly isn't it?

MRS HARTE   It is.

GERARD   Come back with me, please. Let's run away together, you and me.

MRS HARTE   Don't talk so soft.

GERARD   I'll never give you up.

MRS HARTE   What?

GERARD   I'd be afraid to.

MRS HARTE   You might have to.

GERARD   No have to. I can order experience in my nut if I want to.

MRS HARTE   You'll soon get snapped up. Come here. You're going grey. I had two or three children when I was your age.

GERARD   I'll never give you up.

MRS HARTE   Don't talk so soft. You'll get snapped up.

GERARD   I'd be afraid to.

MRS HARTE   You might have to.

MRS HARTE   I watched it. I would have helped had it been possible. I would have stopped had I known in time. Had one known one would have, don't you think? I wouldn't have wanted it would I? But I watched from a good seat going through much the same myself.

MRS HARTE	When you ran away.
GERARD	What?
MRS HARTE	You ran away.
GERARD	I didn't run away.
MRS HARTE	For hours it seemed.
GERARD	I'll run away from you.
MRS HARTE	What?
GERARD	You said it often enough.
MRS HARTE	I should have done, that's what I should have done, run away from all of you.
GERARD	I'd like to run away from all of you.
MRS HARTE	What?
GERARD	That's what you said.
MRS HARTE	When you ran away I was so frightened.
GERARD	Don't bring all that up. I only went over the tide.
MRS HARTE	You slammed out of the house.
GERARD	I walked over the tide, I forgot.
MRS HARTE	For hours it seemed.
GERARD	I never said I'd run away.
MRS HARTE	I thought you meant it.
GERARD	I never said I'd run away.
MRS HARTE	You did.
GERARD	It was you.
MRS HARTE	Now you've run away for good.
GERARD	Mam.
MRS HARTE	Yet there was a time I couldn't move without you round me grizzling.

GERARD	When I first come back...
MRS HARTE	What are you saying?
GERARD	When you were first ill I needn't have come back.
MRS HARTE	What?
GERARD	I wasn't writing.
MRS HARTE	You didn't write much.
GERARD	That's what I said.
MRS HARTE	You came back quick enough when it suited you. You'd better go back I think.
GERARD	I wish I hadn't come back, I can tell you. I wish I hadn't left to come back, I wish I hadn't been here to have to come back, I can tell you.
MRS HARTE	Oh that's nice. You needn't come back. On your way brother. Pack your bags, mate. What do you think I've got to keep you on.
GERARD	What are you talking about? What are you talking about?
MRS HARTE	You'll be the finish of me, you will.
GERARD	You'll see to that, won't you?
MRS HARTE	You're a bully and you always have been a bully. What did you come back for? Go away. Leave me alone. What have you come back for?
GERARD	Because you're the only thing I have to show off with. You're the only thing that contents me. You're the only thing I have. That's all I have. It's all I have. You're all I have.
MRS HARTE	If anyone's heart's broke, it's mine. And to think there was a time I couldn't go to the toilet without you banging on the door.
GERARD	She doesn't exist. Not so long as she's in here. But she's pushing her way out as her fear becomes my

hysterical talk. She pushes her way out so I clench my teeth. She pushes against them. Eases through them and I can't close them. They're aching.

GERARD	Look out the back. Look out the back.
MRS HARTE	What?
GERARD	Look at it. Why don't you clear it up? Why don't you? Why don't you?
MRS HARTE	Why should I?
GERARD	Why shouldn't you?
MRS HARTE	God give me patience.
GERARD	Why?
MRS HARTE	I'm sick of it. I'm sick of it. I'm sick of it.
VINCENT	Mrs Harte?
MRS HARTE	Who's that?
VINCENT	It's me.
MRS HARTE	Who's that?
VINCENT	It's me, Mrs. Harte.
MRS HARTE	Vincent. Come in, Vincent. What is it? Gerard's out. I don't know where he is. I haven't been in long myself. Haven't you seen him?
VINCENT	No.
MRS HARTE	He won't be long. At least he shouldn't be long. You wait till he *does* come in. Sit down, son.
VINCENT	No thanks.
MRS HARTE	And if you're going out the pair of you be in a bit earlier. Sit down, Vincent. He won't be long.
VINCENT	Do you think you could...

MRS HARTE	What, love?
VINCENT	I think the door's stuck. I can't get no answer.
MRS HARTE	Where is she?
VINCENT	The door's stuck. I can't get no answer.
MRS HARTE	Where is she? Vincent. Vincent!
VINCENT	She's in the...
MRS HARTE	Vincent.
VINCENT	She's in the...
MRS HARTE	Where?
VINCENT	In the...
MRS HARTE	When I did go in, I called and called. Then I got the oldest girl to take the other children down their aunt's. I kept the baby with me. Where is she? What is it? Where is she?
VINCENT	She's in the...
MRS HARTE	I'll go in. You stay here. Gerard won't be long. When I did go in, I tried the door, but I couldn't get it to budge. So I had to get a hammer to it. Mrs Driscoll!
GERARD	He-llo! You in here?
VINCENT	Yeah.
GERARD	Where's my mother? Is she in yet? I'll get murdered. I said I'd come straight home. Where is she? What's the matter?
MRS HARTE	Mrs. Driscoll.
GERARD	What's the matter?
MRS HARTE	I couldn't get the door to budge. I tried forcing it. But I couldn't get it to budge. So I had to get a hammer to it. Mrs Driscoll! Sheila!
GERARD	Your mother's having a baby, I think.
VINCENT	She is not.

GERARD	She is.
VINCENT	She is not. How would you know?
GERARD	My mother told me.
VINCENT	She did not. She is not.
GERARD	She is. I heard her tell my mother.
MRS HARTE	She wasn't a great deal younger than me . . . silly girl. Oh she was a nice girl. A really nice girl. She didn't look any different, except for the burns on the side of her mouth.
GERARD	You coming out after?
VINCENT	No.
MRS HARTE	Come on now, Mrs Driscoll, love. Mrs Driscoll. Can you hear me, dear? Perhaps if I'd been in earlier? No.
GERARD	Or, come on.
VINCENT	Shut up you.
MRS HARTE	So I had to get a hammer to it. But I couldn't find one.
GERARD	What's the matter?
VINCENT	Oh shut up you.
MRS HARTE	Where's the hammer, Gerard?
GERARD	I don't know. What d'you want a hammer for?
MRS HARTE	Where the hell is it? Where's your father?
VINCENT	He's still in work, I think.
MRS HARTE	Where's your father?
GERARD	I don't know.
MRS HARTE	Go on out the two of you. Go on. Go on out. Out.
VINCENT	Mam.
GERARD	What's the matter?

MRS HARTE   It doesn't matter.

GERARD   What's the matter?

MRS HARTE   Be quiet you. Where the hell is it?

VINCENT   Let us in, Mam.

GERARD   What is it, Mam?

VINCENT   Mam.

GERARD   Mam?

MRS HARTE   What?

GERARD   Don't go in there.

MRS HARTE   Why not?

GERARD   I don't like her.
VINCENT   Mammy!

MRS HARTE   What do you mean?

VINCENT   I can't get no answer.

MRS HARTE   Gerard. Run down the Presbytery. Damnit all. Go on. The both of you. Go on. Mrs Driscoll! Mrs Driscoll! The oldest girl went to live away. He kept the others except for the baby, who went down the auntie's. The oldest boy went to sea. I got splinters in my arm breaking down the door. I brought the baby in with me. I'll bring the baby in here Vincent. I've sent Eileen down your auntie's, love.

GERARD   What's the matter?

VINCENT   Eileen went to live away. *He* kept the others except for the baby who went down my auntie's. I went to sea. I see him shuffling round. I got a place when I come home and got them all together. They're all married now. I see their kids. I suppose you think an injustice has been done. To him, I mean, he still works. No he doesn't. He's given it up now. I can't fathom out when she exactly decided it. She give me a note for the chemist. For some cleaning stuff. He wouldn't give it to me. Then he did. Poor bloke.

MRS HARTE Then he went to sea I think. I don't know whether it was the Merchant or the Royal.

GERARD It was the Merchant. It was the Merchant.

MRS HARTE Poor man.

GERARD Who?

MRS HARTE Him next door. He was all right. He was a quiet enough bloke.

VINCENT He was about nine and he was dancing about.

MRS HARTE I brought the baby in with me.

VINCENT Coming out, Ger?

GERARD I can't, she won't let me.

MRS HARTE Then he died.

VINCENT I was cold.

MRS HARTE Oh well.

VINCENT So I went indoors.

MRS HARTE He was a lovely boy. He was lost at sea.

GERARD In the other photograph are other children. None of them is me.

MRS HARTE I scraped all my hand. I got splinters all up my arm.

GERARD Look at the sky.

VINCENT Dear Daddy, I hope you are well, that you are in good health and that it's all right where you are. Dear Daddy, I wish you were home. Dear Daddy, I wish you could come home for good. I hope I'll get another postcard again. We all got our cards and we hope you got ours. Lots of love, your son till death – John Vincent O'Driscoll.

TWO

GERARD   He was sitting opposite me. I look like my mother in
          every way except for the hair, he said. It was New
          Year's Eve. We smuggled two bottles of whiskey into
          the squadron cinema with us. We'd already finished
          the other bottle. Or rather he had, really. I was
          attached to a Scots regiment and it was New Year's
          Eve. We drank from the neck, turn and turn about
          and then out of bravado he opened his mouth wide
          and poured nearly half a bottle down his throat and
          then he pulled my head back and tried to pour some
          down mine. I laughed and choked and giggled. We
          slumped back, our knees up against the heads in
          front, knees against our heads, heads on shoulders
          and shoulders supporting heads. We watched the
          film shouting and drunk. We'd all seen it before.
          Once that week. We were soaked with sweat. The two
          fans in the tin roof didn't make a blind bit of
          difference.

VINCENT   It was very cold. He could have only been about nine.
          I could have watched him for hours, dancing about. I
          chuckled, he was so comical. He was having the time
          of his life. But it was cold. So I went back in by the
          fire. I was in digs at the time. Down Grange I think.

GERARD   We were shouting, greeting people, yelling happy
          New Year to people as we made our way down the
          main road. Who shouted and greeted us. Groups and
          pairs singing and shouting, arms around each other.
          Fighting. Two squaddies fighting quite viciously,
          slogging away covered in dust. We wandered under
          the verandahs of the officers' quarters, and saw one or
          two poor bastards trying to sleep in their rooms,
          turning under their nets. Humourless bastards. We
          walked along the broken floors of the abandoned

section near the boundary. Empty rooms. Mesh
doors banging. Sand filling some of the rooms almost
up to the ceiling. We sat down. He sat opposite me.
You've got hair just like my mother he said.
Grabbing. Where did you get it? I told him. Oh
Jesus, he said. So we lay on the steps for hours, half
talking, half singing, half sleeping.

VINCENT   She left cupboards and cupboards of clothes. Silk
blouses and silk dresses. Hangers of them. And
drawers of under-clothes and stockings. Pale silk
underwear and silk stockings with seams. And shoes
and bags and scarfs. And handkerchiefs tucked away
in drawers ... And we found shoe boxes full of letters,
love letters, and our birthday cards and a locket with
hair in it and a little white baby shoe even, and old old
cards. Couldn't have been hers, with lace edges. And
the stink of scent and powder. We had to live with it
months after her.

GERARD   She left jewellery mostly. Rubbish really, but very
pretty. Trinkets really but some quite nice pieces as
well. A crystal cross I liked. Nothing very much. A
clip I liked and her rings and of course her books and
drawings. No money of course. Very little. Well
hardly any really.

Prolonged laughter from Vincent and Gerard

VINCENT   We practically had the nine o'clock run.

GERARD   Did you...

VINCENT   Do you...

GERARD   Was it... Were you... Did we...

VINCENT   When you... When I...

GERARD   Were you... Did you...

Gerard opens his mouth to speak again but can't

VINCENT   Speak up.

MRS HARTE	I got your magazine. The flowers I gave to one of the women who was very ill to cheer her up. The other woman and myself had a room to ourselves in the convalescent home. You'd think we were staying in the Ritz. You've no need to come home you know. You don't look well. Don't think too harsh of me will you? You saved my reason. Nobody don't know nothing about all that money. Don't say anything will you? Is that why you've come back?
GERARD	Of course it isn't.
MRS HARTE	Oh come back. I'll look after you. Don't cry. I haven't been out since last week, so that's cheerful. I haven't seen anybody. Ah you're the best of the bunch. I'd sooner put paid to myself than ask anything of any of them. Don't be unhappy. You've been no disappointment, not even a worry really. You're a good boy. Don't be unhappy. I may have been wrong and no doubt I'll have to pay for it ... but don't be unhappy.
GERARD	Where are they? You've been taking sleeping-tablets during the day.
MRS HARTE	I haven't.
GERARD	You have. Look at you. Listen, you've got to change. You've got to. You're killing me. You've got to stop.
MRS HARTE	I've only had a bottle of Guinness.
GERARD	I know. I can smell. You can hardly stand up. You've got to change.
MRS HARTE	Don't be silly. I'll be all right.
GERARD	You've got to change. Damn it all you've got to stop. You've got to leave me alone.
MRS HARTE	Don't.
GERARD	You must. Listen to me. You've got to. Are you listening, Mam?
MRS HARTE	I'm listening.

GERARD	You've got to. Why don't you stop?
MRS HARTE	Don't be foolish. Now leave me alone.
GERARD	What's the matter with you, eh?
MRS HARTE	Nothing.
GERARD	What's the matter with you, eh? What is it you want? Come on what is it? What do you want, Mam?
MRS HARTE	I'm paying dear for any wrong I did in the past.
GERARD	What is it? What is it you want? What do you want?
MRS HARTE	There isn't anything I want, only peace of mind.
GERARD	Oh...
MRS HARTE	Ssh... Listen.
GERARD	What to?
MRS HARTE	Sh. Sh. There's the train. Whenever I hear a train I want to be on it. I don't know what we moved for. I never liked it here. I had lovely neighbours. Lovely folk weave curtains. I miss that back-to-back grate.
GERARD	I was ashamed of you. Utterly. Of myself. Utterly.
MRS HARTE	Are you any better?
GERARD	Of course.
MRS HARTE	I wish I could come up when you're like that.
GERARD	No, of course not, of course not. Of course not. I've been desperately trying to die ever since you, I don't know the date. When was it? Ever since you decided it. I've hundreds of letters from you. They're all about nothing but you haven't any money. Money. Money. Money. Money. Money. Money. Money. Money. Money. Can't you manage?
MRS HARTE	No I can't manage, anything.
GERARD	You can't manage anything. You've got to stop. You've got to become who you're supposed to be,

who you told me you were, they told me you were,
you believed you were. I know who you are. It's not
good enough. I've become what? An imitation of
what you're not actually yourself. You had better die.
There's got to be a moment. Do you remember it? I
saw you decide it was all up for you, I observed eating
the side of that cream and green pram. Do you? Do
you, eh? You had better die.

MRS HARTE   I don't want to die! I want to take part. I don't want to
be one of those old crows who've grown old
gracefully and go with dignity when their time comes
because they can't bear what's going on because they
know they've got no control of it. I'm afraid to die. I
must be hard. I don't think so.

MRS DRISCOLL   How are you then?

MRS HARTE   I'm fine. I've got the kettle on. Thank Christ for a sit
down.

MRS DRISCOLL   The baby's out the front asleep. Michael's took
himself down our Julie's.

MRS HARTE   And mine are out till dinner time. Let's sit down for
Christ's sake. Thank God for those back-to-back
grates.

MRS DRISCOLL   I'd say.

MRS HARTE   I've got the kettle on it. It saves me a lot in coppers. I
thought I heard Vincent.

MRS DRISCOLL   Yes. He's gone down the shop for me. He's been
home since last Wednesday week. He'd a kick playing
football and he forgot to go back.

MRS HARTE   So that's cheerful.

MRS DRISCOLL   He's got me heart scalded. I told him to stay in
school. But no. And now he don't want to finish his
time.

MRS HARTE	Well, it won't be worth the time he has spent.
MRS DRISCOLL	You try telling him that. I've been up since six.
MRS HARTE	What for?
MRS DRISCOLL	I don't know. I've been working.
MRS HARTE	You're better today. You look better.
MRS DRISCOLL	I am. I feel better.
MRS HARTE	*He's* got a cold and is happy as ever can be.
MRS DRISCOLL	I brought the paper back.
MRS HARTE	Thanks.
MRS DRISCOLL	I see Churchill's gone on holiday.
MRS HARTE	Yerra he's been on holiday all his life, that fella. Bloody warmongering bloody old get. Bloody cigar. I hate low men.
MRS DRISCOLL	I see they've painted Nye for Prye on the bridge.
MRS HARTE	Oh him, bloody Communist bloody get. Ah well. *She sighs*

Mrs Driscoll begins to sing. Sweetly

I haven't heard that for years. *She whistles and joins in with phrases she knows* Come on.

MRS DRISCOLL	What?
MRS HARTE	Up you get.
MRS DRISCOLL	I can't lead.
MRS HARTE	Nor can I. Hang on. Here we are. *They dance. Very well. Singing and talking* What is it?
MRS DRISCOLL	I don't know.
MRS HARTE	My Christ, when did you last have a dance?
MRS DRISCOLL	I don't know *They laugh* Look out there.
MRS HARTE	What?

MRS DRISCOLL   That old fella up the top. He can't believe his eyes. We'd better stop.

MRS HARTE   What for? Let him look. *They dance on until Mrs Harte stops* Christ. There's the door. It's the clubman.

MRS DRISCOLL   Well he knows I'm in. The baby's out the front.

MRS HARTE   Well you're not there. You're in here. Come on out the back door and into Mrs Wallis's before he twigs. She's got different callers.

MRS DRISCOLL   Just my luck if Vincent is coming up the street.

MRS HARTE   If Gerard comes out of school early, I'll blind him.

GERARD   I'm exhausted looking out of train windows. No sense but sight, no touch or scent, so that one can't smell or feel. Silent as film dissolves. Better the train's smell, the train's noise, the city view, the townsman's countryside. Pan is locked up in this train and panic. No apocalyptic vision of the nineteenth century. No smashing through the sunshine past red brick mills and factories like cathedrals. Last glimpses, all like last glimpses. A need to feed and record. The need, but no accurate recording apparatus. It's like eating without chewing. Last glimpses. Broken stone, broken pram, broken tractor, broken lorry, broken wood, broken iron, broken car, broken bike, broken water, broken tiles. A boy in red. Boys' arms around each other. Council, fields, houses, paint on walls, broken sentences, broken chair. Pulped cars, mashed, piled high, like pulped metal paper, giving nothing to the future. Skirt cities. Outside they leave behind things to grow over with seeds of the country. They've run to seed. Old train terminuses with broken platforms. Like being on a ghost train this. Lovely as graveyards can be, ones that they're going to knock down and run roads over, as ones that are going to be run over by cars, hundreds of cars. Buildings are overgrown like the countryside itself is overgrown. Domesticated, turning them into follies. Don't kill the chance of beauty. This beauty. Collected like junk in the country's attic. They have their meaning I'm sure. On we zip, the ghost train through other stations and halts. Then the red starts. Dark, dark red. The berries are huge, there was no frost in the spring. Birds are the only wildlife in this countryside. One magpie. Two for joy. So much red it seems like an obsession, so, observe. It's not an obsession. Obsessive about what is there. So many berries and bushes, the greens and reds mixing, each losing its intensity, defocused, mixed so to speak, defocused, confused by their intensity and this speed. Thick with berries like ampoules of oil. The reddening reminds me of harsh winter afternoons with willows reddening in the spring. Red September. Hydrangeas soaked in red. Some trees starting to gleam, glowing, passing, fail and then glow. Single trees like these are creating aureoles in woods. Llanwern turning red with dust. Miles of blue laminated boxes under red dust. The green between the two towns has hedges, they're red. Red pullovers on lovers with a dog, one red arm round another red shoulder. The reens are covered still in their slime. Pulling in, past the old town, the Dowlais, the old works is chalked in red madder on a blue ground. Hiding in the smoke but not lost to view. Arrived in Argos, experience the bus service and all the impelled feelings are disgruntled and litter ridden.

VINCENT	What you home then for a couple of days like, I suppose?
GERARD	Aye. That's right.
VINCENT	I've come over here for a pint. Where you going?
GERARD	Nowhere.
VINCENT	When you going back?

GERARD	Monday I suppose. I don't know. I don't have to go back Monday . . . I don't know when I'm going back
VINCENT	Aren't you working?
GERARD	Yes.
VINCENT	Do you fancy a drink?
GERARD	No thanks.
VINCENT	It's not a bad pint over here. I'd rather have a pint in a pub though, any day of the week. I don't like clubs Though it's not a bad pint over here.
GERARD	It's too full of people for me. People I can't hardly remember or people who can't remember me, on people I don't know who keep on talking to me, on people I do know, but whose names I've forgotten, on people I don't want to know anyway. It gets too crowded for me.
VINCENT	I sit quiet, me. Down the other end. Mmm?
GERARD	No thanks, I'm not drinking.
VINCENT	O.K. All my *old* haunts have been ruined or pulled down.
GERARD	In town?
VINCENT	Yeah. Or been pulled down. I used to drink in the North and South. That's been pulled down. The Packet's been ruined, the Gun's full of students. I used to drink a lot in the Tredegar one time.
GERARD	Oh aye.
VINCENT	That's been pulled down.
GERARD	It isn't, I passed it on my way home.
VINCENT	No, the Tredegar up Bute Terrace.
GERARD	Oh aye, I saw they'd closed it down.
VINCENT	Yeah. You can't get a decent pint anywhere.
GERARD	You sound like an old man.

VINCENT	Yeah. Sometimes when I'm waiting for the bus I think Christ I'm getting like all the old men up the station running to catch their last bus home to Christ knows what hole.
GERARD	Do you know, I imagined you were still at sea.
VINCENT	What? No fear.
GERARD	Didn't you like it then?
VINCENT	I haven't been to sea for years.
GERARD	Don't you miss it then?
VINCENT	I don't know. You seeing your old man?
GERARD	Yeah.
VINCENT	I haven't been to sea for years.
GERARD	Ay, do you remember Mrs Dwyer?
VINCENT	Who?
GERARD	You know.
VINCENT	I don't know.
GERARD	You do know.
VINCENT	I don't.
GERARD	You do.
VINCENT	The woman with her hair in pipe-cleaners?
GERARD	Yeah.
VINCENT	Blimey.
GERARD	She still has her hair in pipe-cleaners.
VINCENT	Does she still like a drink?
GERARD	I don't know. Anyway I saw her the other day. She had her arm in a sling.
VINCENT	She still likes a drink then.
GERARD	No, that's it. I said, How do you do that, Mrs Dwyer?

VINCENT	What did she say then?
GERARD	She said, You wouldn't mind if you did it drunk, she said. But I got it falling out of church.
VINCENT	Oh aye.
GERARD	How do you fall out of church?
VINCENT	Same way as she falls out of the Moorland. Blimey she must be getting on.
GERARD	Aye. Ey, Mrs De-wyer. Cun we' av ou' borl back?
VINCENT	I got chucked off the altar because of you.
GERARD	I got chucked off the altar because of you, you mean.
VINCENT	That was after you got me chucked off. How long you been home then?
GERARD	Why? A fortnight. I should have gone back last week I suppose. I'll go back on Monday. Though I don't have to go back. I don't know when I'll go back.
VINCENT	How's your old man?
GERARD	Don't you think about it at all?
VINCENT	What, going to sea? Nah.
GERARD	Don't you miss it?
VINCENT	How is he? Funny thing I saw my old man not so long back.
GERARD	Oh yeah.
VINCENT	Oh my old man was great you know. He was. We had some great times. I remember us going out once. Or even twice. No. Fair enough. He worked hard.
GERARD	He worked on the dock didn't he?
VINCENT	He did. He was a scruffer.
GERARD	What's a scruffer?
VINCENT	Well might you ask.

GERARD	What?
VINCENT	What a scruffer is.
GERARD	What is a scruffer?
VINCENT	He shacked up with some blonde piece. In fact he's still with her. Poor old bugger. I can't blame him. He's stuck with her. Or she's stuck with him. He give her the run around for years. First one and then the other. He must be donkey rigged, like me. Ha. I saw them the other week. He didn't see me. He was half boozed. And her. She was stuttered, she was. You should have seen her face, blimey. And her hair. To match. He was walking ahead of her.
GERARD	Where was this then?
VINCENT	In town.
GERARD	I was in town.
VINCENT	Today? Did you get caught in the rain?
GERARD	When?
VINCENT	Earlier on.
GERARD	No, was it raining? I must have been home by then.
VINCENT	It bucketed down.
GERARD	Were you in town?
VINCENT	Yeah, I was flying me. I rushed into the Wyndham Arcade. Then I got a lift off of a mate of mine.
GERARD	So you were all right.
VINCENT	I should say. Barney Williams. You don't know him.
GERARD	You wanna watch you don't catch a chill.
VINCENT	Aye.
GERARD	Yeah.
VINCENT	I'm surprised you didn't catch it over here. It must have been just in town. Don't you fancy a drink?

GERARD	No thanks.
VINCENT	I can't hardly believe I was at sea at all sometimes. I must have enjoyed it too much. Are you sure?
GERARD	Positive. Honest.
VINCENT	Do you know the only proof I've got is the tattoos on my arms.
GERARD	On your arms?
VINCENT	Yeah.
GERARD	You'll get murdered.
VINCENT	Only on my arms.
GERARD	I went with a Scotch bloke once to get tattooed. Thank God I changed my mind. He didn't. What's it say?
VINCENT	Mum.
GERARD	Mum!
VINCENT	Yeah. A crowd of us went after a piss up. In the Mediterranean somewhere. The Canal I suppose. I tell a lie. It must have been. Or was it, it must have been. They say you get tattooed three times. First your mother, then your girl, then your wife. I just got the two.
GERARD	Who's the other?
VINCENT	Jan. And I haven't seen her for two years. Took the baby and fucked off. Mind you I can't be much to live with. Let's go for a drink. Coming for a drink?
GERARD	No.
VINCENT	She always wanted to go out. Skittles. The club. The fruit machine. Or talk. I couldn't talk. *She* couldn't talk. Just a stream of the most effing stupid things she'd picked up. And I'm no bloody good with my hands. Well I could be I suppose. I used to be. But I got no application. I'm not working a seven day week

and then coming home making fitted fucking cupboards. She had lovely dark hair but she dyed it black all the time. So it was sticky. She had ... She ... I can't be bothered now. They hang about me sometimes. I'd sooner use the pros up Bute Terrace if I'm pushed. Outside the Key Beck. Then there was the fuss about him being brought up a Catholic and all that. As if *I* cared. Particularly after the fuss over my mother's funeral. She agreed. She should have stuck by it. I can't think why I made such a fuss now – it doesn't make a blind bit of difference to me. Don't you fancy one?

GERARD   No, honest.

VINCENT   Sometimes I'll catch sight of a woman and there's that look. That, that ...

GERARD   I look away.

VINCENT   Sometimes I'll want to give up my seat on a bus. But I can't. Like I saw this young girl. She only looked about sixteen. All made up to bring you down. But she was so tired. So tired. She was holding one kid and she was pregnant, and she had another by the hand, but I don't think it was hers. But I couldn't stand up. I don't know how to anyway. I look out of the window. It's their fucking faces. You want to knock their fucking faces in for looking like that. They filled the East Dock in.

GERARD   I wonder if we were in there.

VINCENT   Oh come for a drink, Ger.

GERARD   No.

VINCENT   Come on.

GERARD   I said no.

VINCENT   You did for me, you know.

MRS DRISCOLL   Vincent.

GERARD	What?
VINCENT	You did, you know.
GERARD	I did for you?
MRS DRISCOLL	Vincent.
GERARD	*I. I* did for you? *I* did?
MRS HARTE	Gerard.
GERARD	*I* did for you?
MRS HARTE	Gerard.
GERARD	*I* did?
MRS HARTE	Gerard.
VINCENT	You did, you know.
MRS DRISCOLL	Vincent.
GERARD	*I* did?
MRS HARTE	Gerard.
MRS DRISCOLL	Mrs Harte, Mrs Harte.
MRS HARTE	I'm sick of it. I'm sick of it. I'm sick of it.
VINCENT	I'm going in.
GERARD	Don't go in.
MRS DRISCOLL	Oh I'm terrified. Jesus I'm terrified.
VINCENT	I'll have to.
MRS HARTE	I'll split you.
GERARD	Go on in then.
MRS DRISCOLL	Oh dear, oh dear.
VINCENT	Don't worry, I am.
MRS HARTE	I'll cleave you. I'll tear you.
VINCENT	You did you know.

MRS DRISCOLL	Mrs Harte.
GERARD	*I* did.
MRS HARTE	Oh, I'm fed up.
VINCENT	He was only about nine and he was dancing about.
GERARD	I know.
VINCENT	I was cold.
GERARD	You must have been.
VINCENT	How do you know?
MRS HARTE	I'm bleeding.
VINCENT	How do you know?
MRS HARTE	Oh, I'm bleeding.
GERARD	In my hospital pain draws attention to the terminal case... All day he's fluttered his arms, let his blackened arms drift in the air. His wife's face is like a cyst. She tries to rest her head against him. He growls like a comic. Her glasses are knocked to the floor. Oh I don't know what he means.
MRS DRISCOLL	I think it's inclined to rain.
GERARD	The three lamps in the ceiling are burning with dry ice. The sun is hanging underneath the old man's bed. The three white lamps are the three moons of the ward. The ward is tropical now and full of difficult beasts. The white globes flood red for night and we can't sleep.
VINCENT	It's no use. It's no use.
GERARD	In her hospital ward. The sadism of a hospital death. Making the dying cough up their lives.
VINCENT	So I had to borrow a suitcase.
GERARD	I walked along the corridors to pass the time. Up the stairs to the doctors' common rooms and found the

notice board and on it the next day's list. Her name
typed on it. You can never be sure you exist in their
minds really. It's odd to find you must exist after all.
It's so real the pain, you don't exist. And then on the
other hand the pain you do exist.

VINCENT	It was too.
GERARD	Arms above her head. Beyond lowering her eyelids. Aboriginal. Girl's head. Wooden mouth. Burnt sienna eyelids. I'm going to be sick. Are you?
VINCENT	I must. I must.
MRS HARTE	Oh I'm fed up.
GERARD	I shall never break faith with her. I'll never give her up.
MRS HARTE	Oh I'm fed up.
VINCENT	I should have. I should have.
MRS DRISCOLL	Oh much better.
GERARD	What you don't realize is that the death of someone who has been wronged can never be avenged on anyone.
VINCENT	He was only about nine the poor little fella. I was cold.
GERARD	I know.
VINCENT	What do you mean?
GERARD	What I said.
VINCENT	It couldn't have been.
GERARD	It could.
VINCENT	It couldn't have been.
GERARD	It was though.
VINCENT	It was when I was living in digs down Grange. I couldn't have been. He could have only been abou

nine. It couldn't have been. He was like a little girl. No, he was pretending to be a girl. He didn't look like a girl at all. It couldn't have been.

GERARD   It was. It was when we were living over the other house.

VINCENT   It couldn't have been. I was in digs.

GERARD   You weren't in digs.

VINCENT   He was only a kid. He was only . . . He couldn't have been more than about nine. He must only have been about nine.

GERARD   That's right.

VINCENT   Don't talk soft. He was younger than you. He was about nine. It couldn't have been.

GERARD   It was. I remember you looking through the window.

VINCENT   I was cold. You finished me.

GERARD   Where are you going?

Mrs Driscoll is singing quietly

MRS HARTE   I'm going to the shop.

VINCENT   Mam.

GERARD   Why are you going up here to the shops?

VINCENT   MAM!

MRS HARTE   Why shouldn't I? Why are you following me?

GERARD   Because I am.

MRS HARTE   There's no need to follow me. Walk with me if you like. Take my arm if you want to. What is it?

GERARD   It's . . .

VINCENT   Mam.

MRS HARTE   Oh, I'm going on.

GERARD   Now stop, stop walking. Stop.

MRS HARTE   What?

GERARD   Now let's get it clear. Straight. Now.

VINCENT   Mam.

MRS HARTE   Hello, Mr. Farrant.

GERARD   What are you waving to him for?

MRS HARTE   Go home. Hello, Mr Farrant. How are you?

GERARD   Eh?

VINCENT   Mam.

MRS HARTE   Go on. Go away. Gerard. Now go on. Stop it. What are you doing? Stop it, Gerard.

VINCENT   Mammy!

                   Mrs Driscoll stops singing

GERARD   Stop now. Now. Now. Let's stop it. Let's get it straight. Now. Now.

MRS HARTE   I'm bad, Gerard.

GERARD   I don't care. You mustn't. You're not.

MRS HARTE   I'll have to sit down.

GERARD   What are you doing? Tell me. What is it? What is it? What is it?

MRS DRISCOLL   It's all right. I'll be out in a minute.

GERARD   This is unfinished. This can't finish.

VINCENT   Mammy.

                   During the last lines Mrs Harte and Mrs Driscoll are knocked to the floor

VINCENT   You did you know.

GERARD   How? How?

VINCENT   Over the Easter holidays. It was raining you let me in on things. You told me things. I saw things.

GERARD	I finished you? And that's all you can remember is it? A wet Easter. On the wet sand. And flecks of coal. And drizzle. Huddling underneath that old pier. You're one of those people who can't remember anything, except what suits them when the time comes, who leave the hard slog of memorizing to people they find a bit quaint. To people who've found out there isn't a moment you can pin it on. Unless of course you're a rationalist and believe in original sin. Is that what you really think then? Nothing before and nothing after. Huddling together under the old pier talking and talking.
VINCENT	No, but ...
GERARD	You said you loved me. You did. I made you. I realized that you did love me. Too late.
VINCENT	It's always too late. That's the point.
GERARD	You said you loved me, then after we went to the pictures. And then lying in bed, staying in your house for a change, the kids asleep in the other corner, and the light outside, whispering and talking and talking. You kissed me to try and show you did love me and I turned away afterwards because ... That's what I want to know, that's what interests me. You kissed me to try and show you did love me, I turned away afterwards because ... Why? Why? What is it? What is it?
VINCENT	Don't ask me. Always come on. Come for a drink. I'm dry.
GERARD	No.
VINCENT	Well piss off then. You're as spoiled as ever you were. Where you going?
GERARD	Nowhere! You belong to me you know.
VINCENT	How do you make that out?
GERARD	Because I say so. That's why. You belong to me. I'm

74

just expressing the ordinary greed. People try to eat
you. They should let you eat them. So that they're not
ghosts with faces you could forget. They're living
inside you. Thinning you out.

VINCENT   Kid, we was only little.

GERARD   What's age got to do with it! You knew. You were the
only person that could have saved me.

VINCENT   Get out. From what?

GERARD   From THIS!

VINCENT   How?

GERARD   I don't know. I gave you everything I had. My
selfishness. I gave you myself. But you couldn't make
anything of it.

VINCENT   Oh but I did. Don't you have no hope?

GERARD   Do you?

VINCENT   I don't think in them terms.

GERARD   I do. I do. I have hope.

VINCENT   Me, I'll just go on living till I wear away.

GERARD   But who am I keeping alive in my actions. Why
doesn't somebody put me down. Kill her by killing
me. Won't somebody stop it. Stop me. Kill. Kill me,
will you. You won't kill her till you've killed me. Why
did you get married?

VINCENT   What?

GERARD   How fucking dare you. Why didn't you tell me?

VINCENT   How could I tell you?

GERARD   Why didn't you find me and tell me?

VINCENT   How could I tell you? How could I? What? Oh, I
should have asked you should I? Should I have asked
you?

GERARD	Yes. Look, *you*. I never asked for it. I never asked for you. Never asked to play with you, go to school with you. Being who I am with you being who you are.
VINCENT	Nor me.
GERARD	It was different for you.
VINCENT	Oh yes it would have to be. You're so different. It would have to be.
GERARD	Listen, *you*, I'm not paying out any more. *I am not*. I'm not taking any more. Who cares if you did it. I've paid out for thinking about all that. Living all that. Who cares if you did it. Did you love her? Did you hold hands? Did you walk in the park and kiss and cuddle and fool about? Hold hands, hold one hand and smoke with the other. Did you? Did you?
VINCENT	Yes and she was ... She was –
GERARD	Go on, you're right she was. I'm fucking glad. You had a baby. Why didn't you tell me?
VINCENT	You don't care about that. I know you. Do you? And he's not even mine really. Kids aren't. Not with women.
GERARD	But did you? Did you? Did you stay awake at night thinking? Did you get up and pull on your trousers and walk the streets and look up at her yellow window? Did you follow her home and look up at her window? Were you sorry and never asked for forgiveness? Did you love me? Wait for me? Want me? Did you want to run away to the haven of your mates? Did you? Did you?
VINCENT	Come on, son, come for a drink.
GERARD	*Violently* Get off.
VINCENT	You O.K.? What is it?
GERARD	If you've got out of the habit of living in the present. Not the hysterical flash of the present, the actual

present, but the present, the present that surrounds us, the present moment. The tangible immanent present they call maturity. If the present's only reality is made up of fictions of other people's lives and if the past is a location that's unsafe... if the past's out of perspective. If the past's... If you've got out of – See... If the past's... In the past sometimes you can locate pain and feel safe in its hurt – it having gone. If it's bearable you're all right, but if it's not and the past was not, the attempt to make a bearable present is made hopeless by keeping faith with the moral horrors of the past.

VINCENT   For Jesus' sake. What's that? That. Eh, what's that supposed to be?

GERARD   Oh, how would you know. You're so stupid! You're covered in psychic fat. Psychic rind. Wrongs. Wrongs. Actual wrongs. Unnecessary sufferings that incapacitate any ability in you to change. For change. For all change. And if these were caused by other people's, dead people's, inability to deal with their present, then the route is circular and if you're like me the future is as fantasied as the past.

VINCENT   Piss off, Gerard, will you?

GERARD   Look, *you* asked me. It's not only pictures of the past that invented me, but the literal past. The images I made of it may make me immature, but there was a literal past. Things happened that couldn't be changed. And you could have saved me. Now it's anything to get out of the present. The hideous flash of the present moment. The white sound. Chatting myself to death. Do you know, where I am they think it's going to come from you.

VINCENT   What?

GERARD   It, I suppose.

VINCENT   What?

GERARD   It.

VINCENT   Well I hope it keeps fine for them.

GERARD   They *do*.

VINCENT   Well they've come to the wrong shop. Who are they?

GERARD   Oh people I know.

VINCENT   Your circle like?

GERARD   That's it.

VINCENT   Well tell them, look it's very late, tell them. The shop's closed. What they don't realize is that I'm a scab. Scar tissue. No blood in it. Do they, whoever they are, think ... They don't think I'm going to *do* anything do they? They don't think I'm going to fall for the three card trick do they? Do they think any of them that I'm going to take any part? Your old man once said to me keep these open and that shut, son. We were doing a job together. He was O.K. A gentleman.

GERARD   I wish he'd said something to me. Your old man didn't say much either.

VINCENT   I don't think he's got anything to say.

GERARD   All he did in my remembrance is clout us once for lighting a fire down in the shelter. But once when I was crying out in the street, he did stop. He never said anything or dry my eyes or anything. But he walked up the street with me, his hand on my shoulder apparently not taking any notice. But I could feel him – I could feel he existed and it was very, very comforting. And when I think now, that's a lot. Humanness. You know where your old man was brought up? That's knocked down.

VINCENT   That's been knocked down, years.

GERARD   Not one street. Not one house where people spent their whole lives.

VINCENT	Don't be soft. People don't think like that.
GERARD	When I was home once. Queen Street Station had saplings growing through the broken windows. Flowering. Couldn't they have left it?
VINCENT	You've got a war memorial mentality.
GERARD	No I don't think so. I just know you could die of ugliness, and that every piece of ugliness you see is connected with more than my aesthetic displeasure. I know it. It's connected with an immense cruelty. Cruelty of every kind. Cruel ideas, cruel policies. It's not me. It's impossible to put up monuments to the dead, there are too many of them, so they're cementing up people's souls.
VINCENT	You ought to be a Catholic.
GERARD	I would be if I wasn't one. What's going to happen though ay? The only decent people I know are actually mad or there's a few like me wandering around abusing freedom. The other people I know are making a few bob out of being disaffected to pay off the mortgage. Or there's a few girls and sweet boys from good homes. They're nice enough.
VINCENT	I'd watch them. I wouldn't feel too sorry for them if I was you.
GERARD	But the shop steward mentality is not enough. It's not enough.
VINCENT	You don't have to tell me, boy. I was a shop steward. You don't have to tell me boy, I'm sophisticated for down here you know. I'm separated from my wife I am. I even had a mortgage. I read the *Wizard* and J. B. Priestley. I've worked on and off since I was fourteen. I've got a trade I don't use. I've been to sea. I spent one winter scraping the dock bottom. I've worked on tugs in all weathers. I've navvied with Irish fellas I've had to beg to stop and for Christ's sake lean on their shovels so's I could have a rest. I

wouldn't vote if they paid me all the stoppages they've ever took back in one lump sum. I've got some moral standards.

GERARD   Well something got to be done.

VINCENT   You ought to become a Catholic.

GERARD   Shut up.

VINCENT   You can only have a sense of humour on your own terms can't you?

GERARD   How else can you have a sense of humour?

VINCENT   If everyone. You and me that is. If we were all to come out of our holes and put our shoulders to the wheel and say Now look, stop this, this isn't nice, calling people old-age pensioners and the like. And put our shoulders to the wheel. You see I don't trust our judgement. You could be putting your shoulder to the wrong wheel.

GERARD   But don't we have to do something?

VINCENT   There you go you see you won't live will you? What you and I are prevents it. You just said. Something'll happen though.

GERARD   It won't, will it?

VINCENT   When I was at sea.

GERARD   You do remember.

VINCENT   You reminded me. It must have been one of my last trips, I'd got my ticket I know that. I just had this feeling of being on deck of coming up on deck and we were ploughing the South Seas and the clouds cleared the moon, and I thought you and me. You said to me once. Look at the moon. You were a soft bloody kid honest to my God. Why's it racing across the sky so fast? You got a bit scared I think. It's not the moon it's the clouds being blown across it. You didn't like that either, you wanted it stuck up there not sliding about like a button. You told me how your old man used to carry you on his shoulders and run, racing the moon home to see who'd get there first. My father never did that. And you said see the moon, and I said yes and you said as long as the moon was there then we were there. And I had to agree of course. You went on and on like a little caged thing. Till I had to agree, not agreeing with one word of your soft bloody attempts to make things permanent but not real. We were by the hedge, by the privet, you plucking, pulling out the privet flowers, pulling everything apart as usual. And one night when I was a seaman I thought of what you said. And I wished I could smell the flowers. So I thought, the moon, while she's there, you and me both. And I wanted to come home. But there isn't any home or love only in here *Touching his chest*. Do you know I don't hate him. I can't blame her. But couldn't she... have left me out of it. Couldn't they have left me alone?

GERARD   I suppose no-one left them alone.

VINCENT   Look, they're tipping over the foreshore. You been ill? I heard you'd been ill?

GERARD   There are more ways of doing it than pills and drink or banister and rope or downing caustic. Some people do it very slowly over the years.

VINCENT   You could say everybody if you want to look at it like that, son. How old were you when we left? Thirteen, fourteen?

GERARD   Sixteen. You were seventeen. We moved straight after.

VINCENT   I've hardly seen you. Have I. Twice.

GERARD   Three times. And once when I saw you and you didn't notice me. I crossed the road. You looked awful. And I was glad you didn't know you loved me because I couldn't love you. You're falling apart.

VINCENT	And what about you?
GERARD	You didn't love me like I loved you. But you *did* love me. You tried to show me in your way. It was really loving of you.
VINCENT	No.
GERARD	It was. But I was too stupid to realize too unspeculative in the way of our class. I didn't realize that if someone *loves* you they could love you. You see having shown you *loved* me, you could have loved me. Couldn't you? Couldn't you? You could, I know. The thing is you've never liked anyone as much as me have you?
VINCENT	*Laughing* No.
GERARD	And I've never loved anyone as much as you.
VINCENT	It's not like that from where I see it. I haven't got your certainty. But then it's me you're talking about so I wouldn't be so sure. I can see all I may have lost in you, son. I realize you're the only person I've ever had any fun with. That you made me understand how deeply mad it all is. But do you think I'm daft? Yes it's all possible. I went to sea for seven years. Anything's fucking possible. I was the cause of my mother pouring acid down her throat. Anything's possible. You've had no chance. I can see that. But you've had something. You can't lie to me. I can feel it. It makes me feel alive. Perhaps you can't live, but you can create life. Listen to me. What you don't or won't or can't understand is it doesn't matter. Love. What you mean by love. What you mean by love. And you won't get your kind of love. Because you won't accept that it's true, that there's got to be some kind of give and take, some kind of basis, some kind of give and take in the ordinary way. You couldn't take this love you want if you won't accept the offer of a drink. I'm not forcing you. Even if that's what it's about. I can't. Come for a drink. I'm thirsty.

GERARD	No.
VINCENT	Why not?
GERARD	I can't. I got to go in. I've got to have my tea.
VINCENT	And me.
GERARD	Or don't. Stay out.
VINCENT	No. I got to go in. Come for a drink.
GERARD	No.
VINCENT	All right then. Go in.
GERARD	Don't go in.
VINCENT	I got to.
GERARD	Don't go.
MRS HARTE	Gerard.

Mrs Harte and Mrs Driscoll begin to rise.

GERARD	I've got to go in.
VINCENT	Come for a drink.
MRS DRISCOLL	Vincent.
VINCENT	I've got to go in. I'm going in. All right?
GERARD	Don't.
MRS HARTE	He was a lovely boy. He really was. After he drowned. His mother couldn't go up for his seaman's pay. It upset her too much. She'd rather do without it. Then if times were bad, she'd go. But not if she could help it. It wasn't pride. No, it upset her.
GERARD	No French irises. No wallflowers, no new potatoes.
VINCENT	She used to weep bitterly grasping the curling ends of her hair and straightening it behind her ears.
MRS DRISCOLL	I fancy it's inclined to rain.
MRS HARTE	He was a lovely boy. Jimmy Harrington. He really

was. He was ever such a comic. He used to see all the shows. Sing all the songs. Get them off to a tee. He used to cut our hair. Cut mine short for me in an Eton crop.

INCENT   Swimming in the dock, light seeps through the heavy suspension of oil in the water. Head breaks through the water. Never thought one would get there. Out on to a raft. Cormorants. Or climb the cranes with Gerard. Pick up little baby pigeons.

ERARD   In the other photograph, there's a deck chair, with some children piled into it. All in white. Standing behind them, leaning on the back of the deck chair is a man. He's quite vivid really. Dressed in white. Hair brushed back. White trousers and shirt with sleeves rolled back to the elbow and white sleeveless pullover and a dark tie. He's graceful, giving the impression of being tall. Like a cricketer, with graceful arms and hands and legs. None of the children is me. Where is she? I suppose, I suppose she must be taking the snap. I can't believe it.

INCENT   Coming for a drink?

ERARD   I can't.

INCENT   Come on.

ERARD   I can't. She died. She's dead.

MRS HARTE   What love?

ERARD   She's dead, she died.

MRS HARTE   Do you want a cup of coffee?

INCENT   Come on.

ERARD   She is.

MRS HARTE   I'll make it with all milk.

INCENT   Gerard!

ERARD   What?

VINCENT	You coming out?
GERARD	Vincent! You going out, Vincent?
VINCENT	You coming out, Gerard?

GERARD   Vincent!

MRS HARTE   Gerard!

MRS DRISCOLL   Vincent!

VINCENT   Gerard!

Loudly, together

GERARD   Try but can't. Won't but can. Will but can't. Shall but don't.

Note on the playwright:

Peter Gill was born in 1939 and raised in Cardiff, Wales. He was educated at St Illtyd's College, Cardiff. He began his career in the theatre as an actor, working in numerous productions for the stage, television and film. During this time he appeared in the films *HMS Defiant* (1962), directed by Lewis Gilbert and starring Alec Guinness, and *Zulu* (1964), directed by Cy Endfield and starring Michael Caine and Stanley Baker. He is most famous, however, for his work as a playwright and director, and is now regarded as one of the most influential writer/directors in post-war British theatre.

Gill's first directorial post came about in 1964 when he was hired by George Devine as an assistant director to the Royal Court Theatre. Here he directed groundbreaking productions of three previously underrated plays by D.H. Lawrence. These productions; *A Colliers' Friday Night*, *The Daughter in Law* and *The Widowing of Mrs. Holroyd*, were largely responsible for establishing a place for Lawrence amongst the front rank of twentieth century British dramatists. It was also at the Royal Court that Gill made his own debut as a playwright with the 1965 production of *The Sleeper's Den*. Gill first directed one of his own plays; *Over Gardens Out*, accompanied by a second production of *The Sleeper's Den* in 1969. Both were highly praised and he was immediately recognised as an important new voice in British theatre. *Small Change*, again directed by Gill, also premiered at the Royal Court Theatre in 1976. Later, Gill would remember his time at the Royal Court fondly:

'You were made to feel special. I was very lucky compared with the young directors of today. It is all so promiscuous now. At the Court I had the chance to develop within a moral aesthetic. It does you good to be with a group of people whose work you admire. You learn from them and then you can reject their values when you are ready.'

It was also in 1976 that Gill was appointed artistic director of the Riverside Studios in Hammersmith. Over his four year tenure he directed a number of highly successful productions including *As You Like It* and *The Cherry Orchard*, which helped make the Riverside Studios one of Britain's leading theatrical venues.

In 1980, Gill was invited by Peter Hall to become an associate director of the National Theatre. In 1984 he founded the National Theatre Studio, which set up a programme of closed readings for new plays performed by excellent casts, creating a fertile atmosphere for the development of new works and attracting a wide array of talent. Thanks to the success of the National Theatre Studio, Gill has been described as 'the founding father of the new play revolution of the 1990s'. At the National he directed four more of his own plays: *Kick For Touch* (1983), *In the Blue* (1985), *Mean Tears* (1987) and *Cardiff East* (1997) as well as another production of *Small Change* (1983).

His plays, often set in the impoverished Welsh Catholic society in which he grew up, are praised for their tender simplicity and realism whilst his direction is renowned for its brave choices and attention to detail, as well as his loyalty to the cast.

He left the National Theatre in 1990 and since then has directed numerous plays both in Britain and abroad. To date he has written five more plays; *The Look Across the Eyes* (1997), *Certain Young Men* (1999), *Friendly Fire* (2002), *Original Sin* (2002), *The York Realist* (2002), and *Lovely Evening* (2005), and a number of translations and adaptations including a new version of Chekhov's *The Seagull* (2000). In 2002 the Sheffield Crucible held a Peter Gill festival which celebrated his life and work.